Force Beyond Lace

Force Beyond Lace

Poems by

Denise Amodeo Miller

The Writer's Den
Buffalo, New York

Copyright 2009 by Denise Amodeo Miller
All Rights Reserved

No part of this book may be reproduced, copied, or transmitted in any form or by any means without the written permission of the author.

The Writer's Den
Buffalo, New York
www.angelfire.com/journal/garyearlross

Several poems in this collection appeared previously, as indicated below:

"Drink! of Lemons and Wishes"
"Booth"
"Pollock's in Love"
Nickel City Nights: Erotic Writings of Western New York

"The Richness of Beef"
Sol Magazine Winter Contest 2007 - Second Place

"Soup"
Empty Shoes: An Anthology of Poems on the Hungry and the Homeless

"Vittles and Tea"
Gulf Coast Poets 2008 Contest – First Place

"Blood Boost Blood"
Sol Magazine Write Now 2008 Contest Winner – First Place

ISBN 978-0-578-02496-7

Dedicated to the families in my heart:

Unit – Mom, Dad, PJ
Created – my wonderful Evan and Ryan
Congealed – more to love
Writing – my strength and encouragement

~All my love

Drink! of Lemons and Wishes

splash my face gently
cool me with your tide
Quench me

mist me with the freshness of lemons
burst open in the palm of my hand
bright and warm with fervent hope
pleasuring my skin and breath

as wood
undulating and porous
moves and metamorphosizes into art
that I want to touch tenderly
knowing Earth made you and that makes you
somehow
more than beautiful

as granules dissolve within your beat
to sweeten acids bite
to take away the heat and give life
to the multitudes of mystery
living in a depth of silent majestic purity

let me taste the citrus fire with puckering lips
trying not to rape you with my desires
but to take what you want to give to me
and you give me
in this heat
unparalleled satisfaction
and resonate within me
peace

Honeyed

your voice honeys my senses
leaving me coated
paw sticky wet
i lick lick lick the sweetness
on my lips
cheeks covered
other paw swipe
lashes thick
my eyes blinded
but my stars shine
my wind whispers
my bees buzz
oh, i lick lick lick the sweetness
of my hair
the halo of my head
where my dreams
render the honeycombs
of royal jelly
and i lick lick lick the sweetness
of my craving
until I become drenched
in golden warmth
to my glistening toes
glutted

Autumn's Bliss

leaves still wet from morning rain
slick stick wet to my bare skin
in clumps of color
brilliant chrysanthemum yellow
lapping over crimson lipstick
kissing my curves and mudding
brown earth
turning turning
in passionate circles
my long hair damp
spreads across my lips
to cover each exposed proof
of my pleasure dance
in this glistening grass
full of freedom
with the endless spins
leaving me breathless

Booth

Sharing your spoon
Chills me with hot soup

Spice enters my mouth
And I am heat as

Your eyes eat my greens
And ginger

And Red wine licks my lips
And more

Enter the hold of the saxophone,
Sweet

Blind to all
But you

The Roots of Desire

Consume my beating heart
with moments of gentle touch
and the soft scent of
spiced peach and jasmine petals
filling me with passion

Our limbs arched showing sinew and steam
sweat pooling in crevices
making tiny lakes of pleasure
warmed with promises

My desire for you looms
I ache
Complete me

Bring this feeling to Alpine moments
cresting on cool peaks
wet with snow

I beg the wind to move me upward
to the heavens
beyond my comprehension
intense and real

And when I can't go beyond
and reach that bliss
revel with me below it
in twisted roots
glowing quietly on the damp earth
in consumable ecstasy
and rare instances of peace

Pollock's in Love

As your mouth opened I saw your flesh
combine with
           colors
and splay my eyes with longing
A multitude of pigments arching toward me
In thick swirls and deep scent
Wet with meaning
And as we meld in our newness
We design a chemistry of artful desire
Mixing with the green of the trees, the heat of the sun,
the damp of the grass
Until you close the distance and our bodies blend into
A brilliance of White
                  White
                        Oblivion

Our Cherry Blossoms

tender shoot
i stem from the seed you've planted
slower i grow than i desire
but sweetly
gazing upon your rich brown earth
flecked with mica

my limbs begin their stretch
taut with spiking life
revel as my leaves unfurl
each vein filling with sunlight
oh, look now as
the bark begins to tense upon my sensitive skin
and i reach and try for more and more
i excite in my strides
filled with brilliance
and joy
i venture ever upward
and reach into your depths
i pull parts of you with me
in my primal journey
wanting never to leave your warmth

resilient buds form
ready soon to burst
from their caring cocoons
in a symphony of pinks

cherry blossoms sprout upon our tree
and we breeze gently
quaking slightly
in their deliverance

soon the lanterns will be hung
red and gold silk slow movement and
mild conversations that will last
until the weary drift humbly
asleep and dream
on the petal laden grass mosaic
that we both have made
more radiant

Dew

the color green was vibrant today

each blade of grass

dripping juice

sweating

like

HOT SEX

down

into the crevasse of mother earth

The Fresh Flesh of Love

soft skin
covered in fine hairs
curving over muscle and bone
in a poetry of flesh
each inch a revelation
of cells
browned by summer
with dark moles scattered like stars
in constellations of you
mapping out our universe
and speaking the languishing language
of soft sunday mornings
in love

Sugar Grain

Sugar grain
Small and sweet
Begins my journey
As it sits upon my tongue
Arresting my senses
Bursting open my heart

You set it there upon your breath
In that one long moment
When you drew me close
For the first time
To taste our chemistry

And that grain is now placed where it
Has been destined
To dissolve my restraint
Though I know it oughtn't

Yes, it sits there
Devil plump with empty calories
Dionysus that bids me taste
Gorge upon grapes and figs
And I may
Only to pray for the rush to be worth
The hangover tomorrow

Think Love

i catch that sense of wonder
in your eyes
as i spread across lean lap
running my fingers through tight curls
and devouring soft lips
sensing that i can't
read your mind but

i can
breathe and sigh
atop your jeans with
taunt muscles below shirtsleeves
in my gentle grasp

i can
enjoy your wiry hairs
as they sense my skin and
your soft hands searching
my back for clasps and

i can
wonder in silence
my lips sealed with yours
about lonely nights
and others' hands but

for now

you are mine
and i want you
open your doors
and let me inside

for now

i'll blind my worry
to feel   woman
and think   love

Lover's Leap

Broken shells upon the seafloor
through shallow water
and the finish of waves
shimmering dots of white
looming in rippled sand
among clusters of seaweed
they display an artful grace
of collage such as
clothes lost upon
the floor
through the night
while lovers' passion is spent
with wet brisk legs
I pass among this mess
my feet wince
not leaving a lasting
impression as I step over
to search for the sun

Shifting Sands

squish between toes
the sand soft
of earth
shifting
moving up
through each curved
crevice
small
grains
rearrange
and form shapes
of tiny towers
cities
now
ruins
flecked with
stone
and
old
stories which
dry upon
my
feet
and blow
into the wind

Sea Gift

beauty in found moments
of sand's scratch
on sodden soles
soberly
upon my palm
turned and warmed
by the sun
sea glass
discovered as jewels
once clear
now clouded
in ethereal luminescence
smooth to skin wet
sliding in
to tumble
as rock
in waves of pleasure
pull my thoughts
into your gossamer dream

Manic Movement

web of manic movement
streaks across my path
the birds have left their mark
of search
desire
need
in frenzy upon the sand
imprints of the moment
they thought this was the place
where cheetos choose to land
breast to breast
soulless glare ever watchful
pecking out an order
yet undefined
only to orange a tongue
designed pink

Wet Pages

It washed up at my feet
among the swirling sand
bringing my toes alert
to its beautiful pink presence
blue butterflies and iris
in shiny smooth plastic cloth
covering wet wet pages
the lines inside smudged
the sea having uncovered their life
tiny pink journal
holding sweet dreams
secrets
emotions
ink-stained and bled out
again
salted tears now not the only
wet it knows
for a time
waves replaced joy and
turbulent emotions are now felt
with more than a pen's weight
the time past dissolved and
usefulness gone
nothing now but waste and memories
discarded moments
but life resumes
without a blink
to our lost little journal

Mosquito Moon

beneath the canopy of stars the
night is alive with mosquito moon
as the hiss of yellow firelight
sings to the beat beat beat of batwings
on a trumpet of tender air

Oh, whispering mosquito moon
please don't drain my precious blood
with your yearning whiteness
and leave me still
with some opalglow
so that I can strive to shine
as you do

The Brevity of a Breeze

time speeds forward
into angling traffic
into conforming lines
into burdened hands
only too happy to continue
on his merry way

but for the tinkling of chimes
which awaken the senses
to the sweet taste of spring
giving fleeting moments of beauty

for the metal joins us in the song of the earth
whose melody entices our hearts
into times of peace
release
within a memory of something

   s   i   m   p   l   e

as those lines that once conform
but now
curve
intertwining
with the supple trees
sundrenched grasses bent with gentle wind
cool rippled mudwater
and wild jackrabbit's jump
into fields strewn with multitudes of color
baking in that sun which
glistens upon the rods that strengthen
and renew
with the brevity of a breeze

Autumn in Buffalo

standing at the water's edge
biting winds make brown sound
smelling of fish and icy temperaments
as the watchful green succumbs to display

in increments

though the color hesitates at times,
since most of the trees are sick
from October storms past
i watch as they falter

black spots growing larger eating up their brilliant color

and within them serpentine mists carry
exhaust fumes of Pierce Arrow
wandering canary fringed parasols aside russet bustle
while colored musicians blow the mooche and the falls
rushes in the distance
wanting desperately to sing along

but it just can't keep up with that wind

down the cobblestone streets
along the waterfront
toward the lighthouse that peers from the great green lake
and remembers the many colored hues

Kiss the Earth

I lie down and kiss the earth
for its graceful hawks soar
its rushing river ripples
for its moist coolness after cold hard rain

I lie down and kiss the earth
for fur that is brilliant in my arms
if only for a moment
of closeness with that small pink nose

I lie down and kiss the earth
for authors of beauty and sorrow
words compiling tension
released onto an escaping dove's back

I lie down and kiss the earth
for Martin movies that infuse my smiles
the buttered popcorn fingers
beside sour candy's bite

I lie down and kiss the earth
for the beaming pride of a win
forcing glory into green eyes
the ultimate effort worth the push

I lie down and kiss the earth
for chubby little feet
each toe a kernel ripe
each movement proof of miracles

I lie down and kiss the earth
for the hug of my mother's arms
her health keeping her back
still her sweet voice over telephone wires

I lie down and kiss the earth
for gatherings in crowded moments
food and wine overfilled
everyone knowing your name

I lie down and kiss the earth
for the sides of shoes brushing
arms oh so gently surrounding
and kisses not far from yearning lips

I lie down and kiss the earth
for the ecstasy in nightfall
my breath released into starry skies
our spirits flying in cool wind

I lie down and kiss the earth
for moments inside moments
for energy and divinity
for labor and love and light

Yes, I lie down
my lips kiss wet with sweat
torrent tears make mud as
the brimful fluids overflow my cup
with life

Oh, Little One

hold my hand
little one
put your faith in me
let me guide you past
the waterfall
so its beauty does not
blind you to its slippery slope
let me run from beasts
who desire you
so they may follow me instead
too hungry to notice the difference
let me jump first across the ravine
dust flying from the earth
and when you're through
we'll brush off our jeans and smile
let me teach you nightshade
from moonflower
the oak not poisoned
to keep you safe and travel far
let me taste the berries
find honey in the hive
rip meat from shattered bone
and feed you feast abundant
Oh, let me do these things for you
so my eyes will shine gladly
watching you glide smoothly
upon the forest floor
forevermore
forevermore

The Tigress Dines

put out a little	piece of heart
and the tigress will subtly	eat
add another piece	to the plate
and she will dine	again
looking at you	with hungry eyes
mmm…another little bit or	more
May I have it	please
so tasty	so full of life
it flows	of caramel
and	clusters
dripping	chocolate
in sweet	spill
Please	Just a bit more

She senses flesh within
her reach and
glances with protective
glare before she dines again
    it is hers
she glows and relishes the
tender tastes

will kill with glee
any who want to sour it
with honey
for there is only
one champion worthy
of her feed
and even then she will
challenge him
to eat with a more ravenous
hunger than she

Force Beyond Lace

Rabbithole Love

save my heart from your rabbithole love
even though i show you how
i crave more quicksand
while i wrap my legs
around your hips
licking your tongue

teach me a way to escape that cavern
even though it's warm and dark
musty with lust
and smelling of citrus tree leaves and
aniseseed bite

i need to be freed 'cause you've told me
it's riddled with stones
stones that you've hidden deep
in the depths
away from my desires

please save me from your rabbithole love
'cause my heart still insists
there must be a redhot lava core
with a luscious treasure room
not all of the others have raped clean

i'm not strong enough so

you must save me from your rabbithole love
i beg you
stop plying me with your tender carrots
knowing all the while
better starved i would be

Blown Away

I gave you my heart and you wore it as a plumed hat
ostentatious and bold
placed atop your circumstance

Yes, I watched you saunter
              down in gibberish town
wearing that fuchsia felt that
you had formed to your skull
giving it your oils
and sweat

That once cherished prop
was used in any way for your gain
and then removed
casually
whenever the wind blew
                        too hard
for it might've been whisked away
ruined in muck

Yet…
you did not truly protect it

You see, that wind blew from time to time
and you held on to that hat
until the day when you decided
you'd had enough
and
     This
was the one that was not
as bound to you

So, if you had to get rid of one
let it be That

Silvered Bells

Ours were plastic so it seems
Molded and shaped
But factory made
A dime or so a piece
At the party store

Nothing to treasure for too long

Just a trinket
To capture a moment
And be thrown away
When life is too cluttered
To bother with such a
Cheap joke

Another Sweet Love

in crisp sea scent
wafting on still warm, musky breath
tender grass brings me from sand
on smoky quartz dreams
in the damp scalene evening

beside me appears
a face
that lulls me into its aloneness
needing me as much as I need

and there together we wander
to watch the diamonds in the waves
that drift upon our aching repetition

a passionate lover's look
sends shivers of silver thread
down my skin, bare and wet
and I cease to breathe
in the hold of those seasalt eyes

as moist fingers
pluck a Clair de Lune with my desire

there, inside me is
this thought of another sweet love
to withhold my solitary suicide
and call me back to bed
alone but with heated hope
through another mistless night

College Cram

i'm not as young as i was
when the night shadows called
whispering of adamant adventure
through the city of lights
when time seemed infinite
and love promising
down at the haunt of sigma delta phi

sleep was a dream and
morning broke open from nightmares
coffee and toast a brief respite from
the drone of overhead projectors
steel cold stadium seating and
pencils that pilfer thrown thought
they pluck a wrap of
overwhelmed words
words that would make or break
your dreams
tunneling ditches and
relieving the dirt of its weight
in books

my mind then
didn't realize the reality
of focus direction and desire
how the sun casts its own shadows
and thirsts
finding in the end it's
too late to travel back
for one last drink

Soup

small bowl filled with noodles
floating in a little yellow sea
sometimes the warmth of you is too good
more than one can bear
pushing love inside my belly
without my consent
but yet I'm lost in your moment
which awakens soft chimes in my gut
and calls open the night
to possibilities

Open the Book

Open the book
and look upon the page
slightly yellowed
dog eared
but supple still

read of all the children
ones your age and not
hold their hands and dance
for a moment again
and feel the silly sun

see mating and lust
arm crooks and other skin
wet and alive
focus drawn on every second
of pure whiteness

see the eyes who've tried
to stain you with knowledge
let your anger weep
for we cannot control others
no matter what riddles we tell

see all the pain and fear
that's been poured upon this page
long nights filled with numb words
rough cut and out of focus
now alive page becomes screenplay

you know
we've all been watching along too
in our own theaters
and the movies are so very vivid
we are tempted to rebend the spine
and shut them out

but keep open the book
keep it open
'cause you just gotta see that part
where the minstrels sing out your life

Boost

blood boost blood
red bubbling energy
for tired cells dying slow
push platelets in bags
to revive some moving
moments of photo album revivals
pallid pinches and laughter
fill sterile hallways
blood boost blood
red bubbling energy
flowing in and out of severs
behind green masks
eyes spill and efforts fly
with prayers and proficiency
to rebuild what accident
took in hazard hells
blood boost blood
red bubbling energy
baby born with dire need
of assistance
repair what went wrong in the womb
quickly quickly
for coo cry to sound
sweet in powdered nurseries
blood boost blood
red bubbling energy
flows through my good veins
let me share it with you
even though I won't watch
your smiles and spins
I feel my own and my loves
and wish you more
sweet simple symphonies

The Richness of Beef

My grandmother's roast beef was chewy
rich with fat and juices
roasted brown with carrots and celery
celery with strings
teeth flossed and tongue tested

Ah, but the beef....
departed and primal carcass
smelling of the porch swing
enveloped in my father's arms
Jumbling the words on paper
dreading the morning
and wishing the meat frozen still

Coverings

The candle burns its wick
The wax pools wet and hot
Pliable and molten
It calls me, as in my youth
Covering my fingertip with spiking pain
Congealing into a shield against the world
Protecting me from the desirable touch

Yet, I am called to repeat the pattern
The pain, the numb
The pain, the numb
Until I can feel no more

I reach for a glass
I can feel its weight
My palm can feel its coolness
But my fingers cannot

I sip at the fire within
Sweet fire of ancient knowledge
But fire soon departs and I am left deadened

Afterward, I look and see
The coverings are still there
The necessary morphing that brings
The bearable painlessness

I want to remove my glove
And I do so, slowly
Looking for the fingerprints I have left

Somewhere

Winter's Roses

how parched we have become
without the moist earth to suckle from
in the dead of winter
our tenderness gone
time has swollen our memories
since Cold cut our tomorrows short
within its pulsating grip necks still sag
steel brown and bleed into our spice red
the dried edges delicately crumble
from saddened heads
and nod to the frozen soil
in sorry sorry winter
only to hope for spring

oh yes
when it finally warms the remnants of our beauty
we'll tumble down among those new grasses
and discover that moist earth once again
to push beyond our death
into resurrection

Stardust Shimmers

on the body of God
stardust shimmers
with the memories that
i pray will never exist to me

appalled He watched as we
starved our brothers
killed them slow
worked them to every bone
wore their golden teeth
whipped them
raped them
crucified their lawns
to decorate willows

in recurring chaos I beg
instead turn women to salt
rather than mutilate them
bring to us
a purge of arkish proportions
to lament our hate
in one final blow

you see
far off
those shimmers seem
angel's tears
and our history
my own

The Second Reader

below a golden sign enticement
compelled by the window
filled with breathing books and
artful pages displayed

the door is open early

depth calls come and wander
come escape the sidewalks pattern
and fill your nose with dusty roses
among pages almost torn
and bordered with green
columns corinthian

beige brown and claret covers
colors more of a stranger's vision
among the markers who hold order
in this lively auditorium and
yellow proclaims their names

abundant first editions
hold the hope of authors'
visions and sometimes
a living honored scrawl
proof of worth indefinable
striking the thought that someday
perhaps your autobiography
will be dined upon too

land and sea
film dreams
poetry metaphysical
einstein's fame
books of childhood grace

sit and admire the bottom shelves
begin to search for one's self in the pages
feeling overwhelmed
all this knowledge turns painful
that we can't take them all home
for easy chairs and tea

i can't write a poem about IKE
you see, i wasn't there
i didn't see it or feel it or breathe it
cozy in my home with my children and my fridge
cable tv to keep me company
how can I possibly comprehend what
those people are going through
floating bodies
homes obliterated
family members lost
can I truly grasp such concepts
never having seen anything such as that?
our storms in Buffalo don't compare
big blizzards blow over in days
roads are cleared and driveways shoveled
but in Texas people will be
bailing
cleaning
building
for months
reliving its horror for years
future grandparents passing worried tales
holding tight to young hugs and hope
nights forever cold at terror winds heals
No, I just can't write a poem about IKE

Among Shingles

What Meaning   there is no meaning to this mess
of wood and cloth on sturdy green grass staring
back bleak at our gaped mouths I see no sign
of God's wisdom here only a shallow note
played low and long to haunt my night
in a stranger's bed with fresh sheets
and towels but not hope 'cause
charity's bittersweet on my
soul Once our home now
debris and gone are the
words to dilate thoughts
into meaning from my
notebook in the
rubble shining
shale shingle
crying out
in meager
voice
me

The Return

bloodhound pup
no longer plundering mowed lawns
waits upon his master's love
and cries moonfully
tears of widows
on broken cement step
nose to nudge ripped screen
upon finch yellow door
trying mightily to
breathe home
only to simper among
the flanked rose bushes
now struggling for beauty
after mangling marauder winds
until the moment of
gravel crunching
and cardoors creak
sounds turned bright
in afternoon rejoicing

Vittles and Tea

feline creature of habit
russet striped and spotted white
with emotion

social above all
                          but you say
no cuddling for you

since you are
too confident in your fur
of days knowing warmth and
an incessant rumbling

run to get your snack

treading upon ceramic tiles
in your loving home

only because I entered the room
you think it time to dine

and so I give in

and watch you as you
shake off that sticky morsel
that doesn't sit quite right on your tongue

we both listen as it falls on the floor

with
            a

                        tap
                                    tap
                                              tap

you glance at it with golden eyes
and decide it is now somehow tainted
so just continue within your feastbowls
of vittles and tea

Give Me a Dream

Give me a dream that will shower me
a dream that will cleanse me of yesterdays
that will caress my limbs in cream
and ease them into readiness

Give me a dream that will melt my mood
a dream that will roux the gumbo
flavors molt mellow and spark
heating my mind for tomorrow

Give me a dream that will race wild horses
a dream that flies in hooves' way
that will challenge the wind
and whip hair in my eyes

Give me a dream that will electrify filaments
a dream that will shock my live wires
creating white light and buzz
scaring my child with fresh memories

Yes, create for me dreams
inspirational and true
Unleash them on me savagely
Surround me with their brilliance
slipping amber sparkles
upon my mind
lingering

Invisible Sunshine

my soul is flecked with resonant memories
and the fear of each unknown moment
asks
will I become invisible
as I stretch outward
toward the sun
will I know the unconditional love of fables
afloat in my heartsong
singing low
in reverberation with the
chant of buddha
this beautiful entrancement
holds my hope with china doll hands
telling me
happiness depends on me
though my weakness for music
depends on you

Midnight Tea

the stars await my visit
to their itchy damp carpet
to sit while they serve
shimmering vanilla cupcakes
scattered upon silver platters
as teacups of floral porcelain hover
and fireflies dance
we gratuitous guests
stay and sip our tea slowly
and laugh long
at the moon's jealous glow

Eve's Fruit

Overripe orchard
dropping heavy fruit
for loose hands to caress and
sing the orbs pulse as
desolate seed encapsulated within
beckons
        "bite"

Why is the Poet's Plight to Suffer?

Why is the poet's plight to suffer
Yet be mystified by the waterfall
Warbling over the smooth wet rocks
Spraying billowing leaves with juices of life?

Why is the poet's plight to suffer
Yet weep at the dawn of a day
Watching soft hued petals surrounding the sun
Waking songbirds to begin morning?

Why is the poet's plight to suffer
Yet see the birth of a child
Hear the cries of delight and tears
And not feel the pain of it?

Why is the poet's plight to suffer
Yet be consumed with passion
Knots in stomach waiting for the moment
Of the desire of a first kiss?

Why does a poet have to suffer
Yet write of life's beauty
Yet write of love
            And nature
                   And dreams
When the suffering itself entraps poetry?
Ah, painful thou it may be
It brings lenses of brightness
Which I place upon my face
And, yes, I wince now and then
But I too can see magnificence
Though sometimes it is off in the distance
A whisper upon the wind

Among Trees

To work, back and back again
Over and over again
Without much more than a glance
At this bench that whispers longingly to me
"Spend a little quality time"
Like my mother's frequent phone calls do

Among a greenbrown dampness I had
Forgotten
      in my cramped but cozy apartment with cable and dvr
Forgotten
      in my mesmerizing computer screen and microwaved soup
Forgotten
      in my laundry chaos and dirty dishes piled high

Now, in just the sound of stoic trees
Of twittering birds
Of footstep's crunch
I find that peace is something I didn't know was even

      m i s s i n g

Grabbing lost lunchbox
Back from the park
Wondering why did it take me so long?
To come back to this
Quiet grass and
Sit

Girl in the Big Floppy Hat

Girl in the big floppy hat
Not knowing where life will take you
Not yet knowing herself
She turns to the bright flash bulb
On a sunny day
And smiles
Holding on to her dreams
Her laughter
Her friends

For that life bolts forth
And rides the rails
Dashes around a corner
Taking the lead
Hold on to that big floppy hat
Hold on through the force of that wind
And ride ride ride
Past the setting sun

Reflections

mirrors are everywhere
mall glass
      car doors
           darkened tv screens
but somehow I don't see   me
in them
not as I am seen in them
I see the me inside
my eyes cloud the rest
but everyone around sees a reflection
that I often forget about and instead
I feel beauty and grace
where it is not in that form
not on the outside
you see
there are times I get it
that fat is not hip
that legs should long
that jowls are not gorgeous
but just a tilt of my chin and it vanishes
and sultry glows and feminine wiles
glare out to blind
my shame

and I am beautiful once again

Unfinished Woman

bring cloth
purest silk and cotton lace
touch it with spandex
for flex and strain
bring it to the table
and stitch it clean

rub your fingers
along the rough edges
feel for loose string
fold them inward
and sew a slender seam
straighter than before

give structure to her curves
fit her ankle with tender hollows
and turn her heel

make for her fitted fingers
for tender hold
attach with button her breasts
and straighten her back

with the last thread knotted
give her the final touches
then set her on her way
to wonder

supple wind

blow on supple wind
blow on
don't fight your nature
no matter how many trees fall
let your wanton lust
seek out unfurled flags
sails and hair tousled
create your art
as you feel it
grind stone
make waves
follow no fools
and chase only dreams
for your gifts are wondrous
and hearttruth
speak them and popcrack
open with their heat
rattle the windows hard
give them their freedom for
winter arrives so soon
blow on supple wind
blow on

Words Worries Wonder

dim lights hover overhead
while my soul empties
on the paper
words worries wonder
dissipate
through to print
dripping their waste
in flow like the flowing hair
spilling over my shoulders

as day dances into night
i will somehow smile serene as
words worries wonder
continue through these poems
without me

www.ingramcontent.com/pod-product-compliance
Lightning Source LLC
LaVergne TN
LVHW011430080426
835512LV00005B/365